Je me souviens

D1416985

Je me souviens

Memories of an expatriate Anglophone Montréalaise
Québecoise exiled in Canada

Lorena Gale

Talonbooks

2001

Copyright © 2001 Lorena Gale

Talonbooks
P.O. Box 2076
Vancouver, BC, V6B 3S3, Canada
www.talonbooks.com

Typeset in Scala and printed and bound in Canada.

Third Printing: August 2007

The publisher gratefully acknowledges the financial support of the Canada Council for the Arts; the Government of Canada through the Book Publishing Industry Development Program; and the Province of British Columbia through the British Columbia Arts Council for our publishing activities.

No part of this book, covered by the copyright hereon, may be reproduced or used in any form or by any means—graphic, electronic or mechanical—without prior permission of the publisher, except for excerpts in a review. Any request for photocopying of any part of this book shall be directed in writing to Cancopy (Canadian Copyright Licensing Agency), 1 Yonge Street Suite 800, Toronto, Ontario, Canada M5E 1E5; Tel.: (416) 868-1620; Fax: (416) 868-1621.

Rights to produce *Je me souviens* in whole or in part, in any medium by any group, amateur or professional, are retained by the author. Interested persons are requested to apply to Lorena Gale c/o Talonbooks, P.O. Box 2076, Vancouver, BC V6B 3S3; Tel: (604) 444-4889; Fax: (604) 444-4119.

NATIONAL LIBRARY OF CANADA CATALOGUING IN PUBLICATION DATA

Gale, Lorena
  Je me souviens

  A play.
  ISBN 0-88922-453-6

  I. Title.
  PS8563.A416J45 2001   C812'.54   C2001-911126-6
  PR9199.3.G254J45 2001

  ISBN-10: 0-88922-453-6
  ISBN-13: 978-0-88922-453-7

Contents

Acknowledgements

I wish to gratefully acknowledge the support of The Province of British Columbia Anti-Racism and Multicultural Program, The City of Vancouver Office of Cultural Affairs: Diversity Initiatives Program, The Canada Council for the Arts, The Vancouver Playhouse, Women in View, The Nanaimo Festival, The Arts Club Theatre, Denyse Beaugrande-Champagne, Pierre Imbert, Leslie MacMillan, Zulus Haddock, Pat Idlette, Michael Luftmensch, Carmen Aguirre, Klodyne Rodney, Fred Michaels, Marlene Franks, Clayton Cooper and King Talent Inc.

Going Home

I used to say that *Je me souviens: Memories of an expatriate Anglophone Montrealaise Quebecoise exiled in Canada* was the articulation of personal memory as political resistance: my tiny dike against the swelling tide of negation and erasure by the thousands and thousands of Parizeaux across Canada who perceive Black or brown people as three-fifths Canadian or Quebecois and would seek to limit our participation in society. However, after three years of performing *Je me souviens*, I have come to understand the work is simply about the preservation of personal memory. It's my crazy attempt to hold on to some of the people, places and things that I love and have lost—my sense of home. And, even though many of these places have disappeared and many of the people, or my relationships with them, have died, *Je me souviens* is my way of saying my brief time with them was formative, important and is still of great value to me. It is my way of saying I love you.

There are times in my adult life when I just want to go home. Not to the home that I have made for myself and my family here in Vancouver but *home* home. My home. Back to Montreal. To my mother. I want to lay my head gently upon her lap, feel the comfort of her crippled hands caressing my brow and hear her sweet voice tell me once again that I am always going to be her girl. Then I would want to go and hangout with my best gal pals at my favorite bar or restaurant, dish the dirt or howl at the moon. *Home*: the one place where no matter how old I get or what I have done, I know that I am wanted and belong.

That Montreal, that home, no longer exists. My mother died ten years ago. My family has since scattered, though my father resides there still. The majority of my friends have moved away to the suburbs, to other provinces or to other countries. Most of my favourite haunts have disappeared from the face of the city. I once knew every crack and crevice of Montreal but each time I go back it feels a little less familiar. I cling to cherished friends who remain and the places that endure like a life raft, afraid that they too will one day disappear, taking the last tangible remnants of my personal history with them. Then what will I have to prove that I once lived and loved and labored and languished in that city of my birth except the memories I carry with me and my rapidly disintegrating baptismal certificate?

It is a legacy of the African diaspora to become rooted to a land where one is always seen as "other." By virtue of my race alone I am immediately perceived as unnatural to my surroundings. Wherever I go in Canada there is a constant demand to explain, justify, and defend my presence. It is as if race is exclusive of nationality; as if the criteria by which we define and measure what is Canadian or Quebecoise could not possibly apply to me. Yet you cannot be born in a land and live there for thirty or a hundred years without it becoming a part of you and you a part of it. The language, the geography, the customs, the rituals, the tastes and the styles all become integral to who you are, even if they are not discernible by others. They cannot help but define you. Identify you. Home is the kiln of identity; the place where all aspects of life and society converge to create that indisputable sense of being and belonging. I need that sense of home to remind me of who I am when everything conspires to tell me who I am not.

I had to ask myself what an independent Quebec would mean for my ethnic family, my ethnic friends and for me. I didn't leave Montreal because of separatist or racial politics but could they one day prevent my return? Would I be stripped of my nationality and identity? Can one be a displaced person in one's own country?

What makes a Canadian? What makes a Quebecois? Is it language? Is it only? Is it history? If so, how long a history? Does it need to have been recorded or can it simply have been lived and stored in memory?

I sat down to write an essay, a rebuttal, a scathing criticism of Mr. Parizeau. Instead I found myself writing down the memories that grew into *Je me souviens*. My childhood, my family, the people and events that influenced me, the experiences that shaped me, for better or worse ... only I can claim them. They are mine. They make me who I am. They can not be negated or denied. It doesn't matter what Parizeau or anybody thinks. Montreal was and always will be my home. I have a living history to prove it.

The wonderful thing about writing *Je me souviens* was feeling that I was somehow preserving my spirit of home. Even better is performing *Je me souviens*: for 75 minutes, I get to go back to my Montreal and hang out with those I love. All the relationships and experiences are fixed in space and time, but that is what home is for me.

Before I left Montreal, my mother told me that no matter how things worked out, I could always come home. And though that place and the people I love belong to the past, with *Je me souviens* I can go home to them again.

—Lorena Gale
December 6, 2000

Foreword

Je me souviens was conceived by Lorena Gale as a performance essay; a theatrical response to the threat of being severed from personal and family history as Quebec and Canada grappled with separation. It is a love poem created in bites and samples from living Black in Canada. It wrestles with questions of identity, alienation and the compelling contradictions within love and longing. It is a theatricalization of a journey of mind, heart and spirit, which ultimately leads back to self and home.

Its theatrical form draws from the worlds of performance art, spoken word, the political essay, the love poem, the cinema, the yearnings of the jazz ballad, the oral tradition of the blues telegraph, as well as the performer's own explorations in "authentic movement" and her twenty-five years as a character actor in the theatre. Experientially, through its multi-textured, multi-form, presentational—sometimes representational—style, the piece operates similarly to Brecht's political theatre.

The audience as active participant is repeatedly drawn emotionally into a world then jarred back into consciousness and processing; pulled back into the viscera, jarred back into the head. The head and the heart are in constant interaction; emotion is given context.

Both form and content repeatedly play off of the notion of alienation. We witness a series of situations where the central storyteller struggles with the alienating effect of being different or perceived as different; the young black English-speaking Canadian child thrust into a multicultural immigrant neighbourhood; the isolated child frenetically dancing to belong; the young woman trying to grasp her mother's litany of dos and don'ts about cultural assimilation; the well-dressed trans-planted black Montrealer trying to assimilate into West Coast Anglo casualness and ultimately, in a series of dream sequences, the storyteller attempt-ing to identify and embrace that distant black dot in a dreamlike and overwhelmingly white landscape. The jump-cut style from scene to scene and form to form, supported by extreme shifts in sound, image, colour and intensity, creates a similar alienating effect in the viewer, heightening our visceral under-standing of each experience and rendering a satisfying form-content relationship. Never sitting long enough in one world to become comfortable, we are constantly forced to experience each event from a new vantage point. This not only provides the fresh viewing which is imperative to all great art, but forces us time and again to question that which we have just witnessed. Having been given such reframed and personal emotional access, we are unable to arrive at the same old answers.

Je me souviens is necessarily of the theatre and demands heightened size rather than naturalism in production. For example, the section "The discovery of what it means to be a Canadian" written in heightened poetic language, is necessarily supported by heightened and poetic physical movement, supercharged slide images and sonically enhanced live voice rising above the forceful yet plaintive jazz yearnings of a Dexter Gordon recording. Elsewhere, a seemingly lost young child is tossed about in a sound bite montage of foreign-sounding immigrant voices or sits overwhelmed at the foot of a monstrously oversized bedroom door, impacted by the size, passion and obligation of overheard late-night voices wrestling with their own adult questions of politics and identity. A young black girl explores a non-black neighbourhood employing the mythology of *Star Trek*'s Captain Kirk. Nostalgia for the sensual texture of Montreal becomes an orgiastic feast of foods and restaurants in a sixties dance party retrospective. The whole piece is, in its own way, a multi-course feast of different tastes and textures, served up with love, by a multi-coloured cast of characters shining out from the writer/performer's own history.

By the end of our shared journey, we have arrived at multi-dimensional picture of a woman having transcended the palpable challenge of being a stranger in her own land (i.e. black in a white world, Anglo in a Quebecois world and Quebecois in an Anglo world.) Through a relentless reshuffling of image and form, the use of Brechtian alienation techniques, the employment of a multi-media production approach, and the juxtaposition of the voices of lost child, loving daughter, passionate freedom fighter, jazz poet and cultural essayist, all balanced by the forward movement of a strong narrative thrust, we are invited on the writer/performer's journey towards self. In accepting, as audience, we begin a journey towards our own selves.

—John Cooper
November, 2000

Je me souviens
Memories of an expatriate Anglophone
Montréalaise Québecoise exiled in Canada

Je me souviens was first produced by the Firehall Arts Centre, in co-production with Curious Tongue and Touchstone Theatre Company in Vancouver in January 2000, with the following cast and crew:

LORENA: Lorena Gale
Directed by John Cooper
Lighting Design by Gerald King
Slide Design by Tim Matheson
Sound Design by John McCulloch
Choreography by Denise Lonewalker and Lorena Gale
Stage Managed by Diana Stewart Imbert

It was subsequently produced by the Belfry Theatre Company, in co-production with Curious Tongue, in February 2000, with the same cast and crew.

Je me souviens was presented as a work-in-progress at On the Waterfront Festival by Eastern Front Theatre Company in Dartmouth, Nova Scotia in May 1998; and at One Yellow Rabbit's High Performance Rodeo in Calgary, Alberta in January 1999.

I

*In the black, we hear music: Robert
Charlebois' 'Lindberg' fades into a few bars of
'This Land is your Land, This Land is my
Land'. The music ends with the sound of a
needle being scraped over a record. The lights
come up on a black stage with a large white
projection screen centred upstage. White
material is arranged in gentle peaks beneath
the screen and extending its length. Upstage is
a white chair. Projected onto the screen is a
slide of Joe's Café in Vancouver. We hear
ambient café sounds in the background.
LORENA enters from the audience.*

LORENA

(speaking directly to the audience) I am on
Commercial Drive, sitting in Joe's Café. I'd
just bumped into another expatriate and,
like those from the old country, hungry for
news from home; whenever we meet we
always reminisce or share news of the
others we have left behind. Its a ritual of
love and remembrance played out on alien
soil by émigrés all over the world. Only
we're in Vancouver and home is Montreal.
The same country. At least today it is.

She moves the chair to centre stage and sits.

We speak in English, my first language and her second. We speak in English because I don't know Greek. We speak candidly, without forethought, without apology. Around us we hear snatches of Italian, Arabic, Spanish, Portuguese, Cantonese, Urdu, et cetera. We speak unashamedly and to each other.

So I say to my compatriot, "I have just come back from Montreal. I can't believe how much it's changed. Everything for sale. Everything for rent. Liquidation. Going out of business. And everywhere those tacky dollar stores. And they're the only ones who seem to be doing any real business. It's sad. I have never seen Montreal looking so bad."

And the next thing I know, there's this long-haired grunged-out French guy in my face saying—

She stands.

—"Hey you! You don't say dat! You don't talk about Montréal!"

He had been listening in on our private conversation, which had obviously offended him, and had half-risen from his seat to stretch across his table and point an accusatory finger at me, like he was the long arm of the Language Police and had nabbed himself another Anglo traitor. He looked irate and triumphant like one spoiling for a fight. My friend immediately put her head down like somebody trying to avoid one. Me ... ? I was stunned into momentary silence.

What could I have possibly have said to offend him? That Montreal looked poorly and depressed? The truth? For a second there I thought I was in a café on St. Denis Street, a little too drunk, voicing my insensitive Anglo opinions a little too loud, and this brave soldier in the struggle for Quebec independence was standing forth to eradicate this heretic from their midst.

I looked around expecting to see a room full of hostile and contemptuous people but no one was paying attention. I was still in Lotus Land. And what did I care since I wasn't talking to him to him anyway. So I told him to "fuck off and mind your own business!"

"Non! You fuck off! It is my business. Me. I'm from Montréal. I know. You. You don't say nutting. Tu n'as pas le droit!"

I don't have the right? I don't have the RIGHT!?

My friend hates confrontation. She tells me to " ... ignore him. He's an asshole. He's just looking for a fight. Come on. Let's go somewhere else."

But I have gone somewhere else. Thirty-six hundred miles to somewhere else. And I cannot back down.

"I don't have the right! Why? Because I'm English? Why? Because I'm Black?!"

"Ah, you. You don't know nutting."

"Oh! Je sais, moé. Je sais assez que toi, hostie. Et si je n'avais rien su, j'aurais eu le même droit de parler que toi!"

"Toi? Tu parles français?!"

"Oui. Je parle français. Je vien de Montréal, moé. Je suis Montréalaise. Je suis née a Montréal. Et j'ai le droit à parler. Le même droit à parler que toi, hostie! Avec n'importe qui, n'importe où—okay? So fuck off!"

"Eh, eh, eh! C'est correct. Je m'excuse. You come from Montréal. I t'ought ... You know, I from Montréal too, eh. And I t'ought ... "

He picked up his backpack and wandered out onto the Drive. My friend was examining the residue at the bottom of her cappuccino. She hadn't said much through the entire altercation and I could tell she wanted to go too. I still wanted to share my memories of Montreal. But the moment was lost. She had to run. And so we parted.

Slide—the rainbow mural on the exterior of Joe's Café.

You know, I'd see him on the Drive, from time to time, with a group of other young Quebecois beneath the rainbow outside of Joe's Cafe. His shoulders hunched from the weight of his pack. His long hair matted into incongruous dreads. He is all passion and gesture and speaks French with a fury so familiar but I can no longer follow. And when I pass he mumbles "salut" in grudging recognition.

We are both, after all, from the same place. His Montréal is my Montreal. His Québec is the Quebec of my birth. Like heads and tails, we are two faces of the same coin. One side inscribed in French. The other English. And we are both so far from home.

I am an expatriate anglophone, Montrealaise, Quebecoise, exiled in Canada. And I remember. Je me souviens ...

Gilles Vigneault's 'Mon Pays' begins playing.
Lights fade out as footlights come up, project-
ing LORENA's shadow on the screen. The
music fades into a dream-like sound, the soft
whistling of wind.

LORENA

Je me souviens d'un rêve que j'avais souvent ...
depuis mon enfance. Dans le rêve c'est l'hiver.
Et je suis toute seule dans une plaine. Une
grande plaine de neige. Y'a de la neige partout.
Autant que les yeux peuvent voir. Pas d'arbres.
Pas de maisons. Rien que la neige. De la neige
qui n'a pas éte defiguré. Immacule. Implacable.
Pure.

Le soleil est un cercle parfait d'un jaune foncé;
suspendu dans un ciel qui est bleu, bleu et
clair. Et c'est froid. Tellement froid. Si froid ...
que ca pique. Et les rayons du soleil sur la
neige ... aveuglante. Je veux rentrer chez moi,
mais je ne sais pas où je suis. Aucun signe de
civilisation. Je suis perdue. Je suis perdue dans
une plaine de neige aveuglante.

The footlights fade out.

LORENA (*as* ETHEL, *a West Indian woman*)
You know what de problem is wit you Canajun
Blacks? You don't know where you come from.
Ya don know who y'are. Ya talk like Whitey. Ya
act all so-so like Whitey. Hell. You even move
like you gotta a rod shoved up to your arse to
brain. All jig-jig like a puppet. And dat's de
problem wit' you. You let the White man into
your head and now you all messed up. You don
tink straight. You Black on de outside, White
on the inside. You're assimilated. Assimilated
Negroes. Dat's what you are.

Blackout. Text is projected onto the screen.

Slide—(text)
When people ask me which island I come
from, I say Montreal. And they look
confused.
When people tell me to go back where I
came from—I look confused.

4

We hear the opening notes to theme from Star Trek.

Slide—family photographs from Little Burgundy, an area of Montreal.

LORENA *(impersonating* CAPTAIN KIRK)
Captain's Log. Star date nineteen-hundred and sixty-one.

We have been living among a small tribe of colored outcasts in an area of the city known today as Little Burgundy—located within the outer perimeter of the downtown central core. Our crew, assembled from Jamaica, Sri Lanka, New Guinea, Bermuda and St. Catherine's Ontario, have spent more than 75 earth years and three human generations in this location. But our work here has come to an end.

May 1st 0800 hrs. We leave Downtown. Traveling at warp speed East along Dorchester.

Slide—Dorchester Street.

North on Park Avenue.

Slide—Park Avenue.

West on Bernard

Slide—Bernard Street.

and north again on Durocher.

Slide—Durocher Avenue.

Successfully circumventing Mont Royal—the pimple local inhabitants call a mountain—in the middle of the city.

We have set a course for Outremont. Our mission—to seek life in new neighborhoods. To boldly go where no Black has gone before!

LORENA *sings 'Star Trek' theme.*

5

We hear a soundscape of voices: English,
French, Dutch, German, Italian, Hebrew,
Yiddish, Arabic, and Russian. They are
speaking in hushed whispers.

LORENA

French filters through as ambient sound and
English is spoken heavily and accented. Our
new neighbor's names are Van Doorn,
Petrovich, Leiberman, Mancini,
Papanicalopolis, Osler, Azra. And each one
speaks a language I cannot understand and
sounds stranger to me than I look to them.

Men with *payos* and long dark coats and fur-
rimmed hats, even in summer, huddle in the
middle of the sidewalk passionately discussing
the Torah in Yiddish. Greek mothers hang out
their windows and holler for their kids, "*Yanni.*
Stavros. Ella thò." Italian men in cotton under-
shirts sit on kitchen chairs drinking wine out
on the stoop and smack their kids for stealing a
sip.

Did we really move across the city or to another
continent?

"Immigrants," my mother calls them, "Beings from another country. Not born here like us."

But no one is like us in Outremont.

They say ...

> We hear the sound of "Go back where you came from" being spoken in different languages.

> *Slide—(text)*
> Go back to where you came from.

LORENA
But I cannot understand them.

6

LORENA

Mr. Camille lives next door. He is a friendly old
man with watery eyes and splotchy red skin
and sits on his balcony chain-smoking Players
Plain and rocking back and forth. Sometimes
he sends me to Finast's to get his cigarettes.
But I am not allowed to cross the street. So I go
up to Frank's, which is on the same side. And
when I get back he gives me a nickel! He tried
to give me a dime once but I gave it back.
Nickels are better. They're bigger than dimes.

Mrs. Camille only wears cotton house dresses
with faded floral patterns and the same tan
cardigan. Whenever you see her she has a
smile on her face but I know ... she cries all the
time. I know because my bedroom wall is
shared with theirs. I often hear her muffled
sobbing, moaning, sometimes wailing on the
other side. She tries to hide it but I can tell.
Her eyes are as red as the smile she paints on
her face.

LORENA (*as a child*)

Mr. Camille? Why does Mrs. Camille cry all the
time ... ?

LORENA (*as* MR.CAMILLE)

My vife. She is not alvays so happy. But vhy
should you care. You are just a little girl. Vhy
vould a little girl vant to know such things.
Vhat can I tell you that you vould understand.

Sits down.

Vhy does Mrs. Camille cry? How can I explain?

Do you know vhat is Holocaust? No. You are
too young to know this. Do you know what are
Jews? Mrs. Camille and I, ve are Jews. Jewish
people. And ve are ... different! Yes. Vherever
ve go in the vorld ve are different. Maybe not so
much here. But ve are different.

Some people in the vorld ... they don't like
different. Some people in the vorld think they
are so much better than everyone else. Not
because they do things that are extraordinary or
good. No. They just think they are better. And
they vant every one to be like them. This, of
course is impossible. But this is vhat they vant.
And if you are not like them, if you are
different ... Then they persecute you. Try to
control you. Enslave you. To kill you.

Ve Jews for many centuries vere slaves. Yes,
just like you and your African people. Ve too
vere slaves vonce. But slavery is not tolerated so
vell anymore. So they persecuted us. Tried to

kill us. All of us. And this is vhat is the Holocaust. But some of us escape.

Lifts up shirt-sleeve and shows wrist.

See? Venever you see this you vill know it was a Jew who escaped death.

Mrs. Camille ... she escaped too. But many, many millions did not escape. Mrs. Camille's mother, Mrs. Camille's father, her sister Yeti, her brother David. All vere lost in holocaust. And that is vhy Mrs. Camille cries sometimes. She cries because she misses her family.

You are a smart girl, I think. Smart enough to ask qvestions. Yes. The answers maybe you don't like or understand so vell. But one day everything vill make sense to you. I vant you to remember vhat I'm telling you. Because you too are different. And it is important that you remember.

These people, who think they are so great. They are so superior. These people are everyvhere! Yes. These bad people are still all around us. Even here. In this Montreal. Today. That is vhy you and me must never forget who ve are. Because ve are different ve must remember. Because if ve forget, it could happen all over again. Do you understand?

Beat.

Good. Now take your nickel and go buy some candy. I have had enough of your qvestions for one day. And don't ask Mrs. Camille. She doesn't like to talk about it. Go!

7

Music begins playing, 'Shaboom Shaboom'.

LORENA

(speaking directly to the audience) Outremont,
Montreal, Quebec. The Sixties. Before *Star
Trek*. Before "Black Power." Before "Say it loud,
I'm Black and I'm proud." Before "Black is
beautiful." Black people were said to have hair
like steel wool, liver lips and some people even
believed we had tails.

"Don't ever let a White man rub your head!"
my mother warned. Like the fat polished
tummy of a Buddha, they would rub your head
for luck.

My mother cleans like one possessed and
dresses me for Sunday everyday. The whole flat
sparkles with a maniacal gleam and I too am
squeaky clean and proper. When she's not
cleaning, she's working; cutting loose threads
and sewing labels on children's clothes
delivered in large boxes to the flat. Or studying
into the wee hours for her nursing exam.

She says they think we are dirty and lazy. So we
must always be careful how we present

ourselves. We must always put our best foot forward and strive to excel excellence. Hard work and cleanliness are the key.

I don't know who "they" are. I don't care what "they" think. I want to play.

She sits.

Instead I sit like Atlas on the balcony and watch the other grubby children on the ground below rev imaginary engines in their Dinky cars, making roads in the dust.

LORENA (*as* LILLIAN)
Don't be asking me to go down there. There is nothing on these streets for you. And I won't have you running around like some wild street urchin trying to find that out. Don't you know that's what they expect from us? You've got everything you need right here. So make yourself content.

Beat.

I know you think I'm being hard on you right now. But you have got to understand. We're coloured and we're living in the white man's world. Don't think for a moment that you can do like they do.

Lights to black.

8

Slide—(text)
HOW TO GET BY IN THE WHITE MAN'S
WORLD.

LORENA

> *(reading)* How to get by in the White man's
> world.

> *'Jazzoid' music begins playing. LORENA
> retrieves a pointer from under the white
> material and moves beside the screen. She
> moves to beside the screen and reads from the
> slide.*

> *Slide—(text)*
> Don't talk back.
> Don't raise your voice.
> Don't wear loud colors.
> Don't do anything to draw attention to
> yourself.
> Smile even when it hurts.
> Just try to fit in.
> And don't rock the boat.
> If any one stops to speak to you, answer
> them politely and only if you have to.
> Otherwise keep on moving.
> Walk like you know where you're going.

Keep focused on what's ahead of you.
If you run into some commotion, don't
stand around gawking.
Don't try to help.
Just keep on moving.
If it looks like trouble is coming towards
you then cross the street.
If it looks like trouble is sneaking up behind
you then run.
If you're surrounded, then fight.
Keep your eyes and ears open at all times.
But if you find yourself in a situation—
don't go to a policeman and don't stand
still.
Just keep on moving and you'll be safe.

*LORENA puts the pointer back under the
white material.*

Slide—(text)
HE WHO FIGHTS AND RUNS AWAY,
LIVES TO FIGHT ANOTHER DAY.

"Nigger" is being whispered harshly in different languages.

LORENA

Outremont, Montreal, Quebec, Canada. We are called "nigger" in two official languages, as well as several unofficial ones. "Black" too is a fighting word. But sounds like "Negro" in so many languages, I do not respond. My brother's fists fly daily.

It is the English slur that is the slur of choice. Even with French kids, who find that "negresse noire" does not have the right rhythmic impact. Anglo, franco and allophone children walk in packs behind you, chanting: "niggerblack, niggerblack, niggerblack," on the way to school. All the way to school. I walk alone.

A loud school bell rings.

Slide—The Union Jack.

LORENA (*as a child*)
I pledge allegiance to this flag and to the Commonwealth for which it stands. (*singing*) God shave our gracious queen. Shave her with shaving cream. God shave the queen. Send her to Halifax. Make her pay all the tax ...

LORENA (*as* MISS BENNETT, *an English grade school teacher*)
Enough. Good Morning class.

LORENA (*as a child*)
(*fidgeting*) Good morning, Miss Bennett.

LORENA (*as* MISS BENNETT)
Open your geography books to page 37. Chapter six. Bunga of the Jungle.

She snaps her fingers and the lights go out.

Slide—a turn of the century depiction of a tribal African.

LORENA (*as* MISS BENNETT)
Bunga of the Jungle. The jungle is a rain forest
located in the Belgian Congo. The heart of
deepest, darkest Africa. Can anybody tell us
about Africa? Lorena?

Silence

Bunga is an African. Africans are little primi-
tive peoples with black skin—Lorena. And tight
woolly hair—Lorena. And broad flat noses, who
run about the jungle naked, climbing trees for
fruit, digging in the earth with crudely shaped
tools for tubers and nuts, and killing
elephants—

*Slide—A nineteenth-century photograph of
African hunters surrounding a dead elephant.*

LORENA (*as* MISS BENNETT)
—with poison darts they blow through long
tubes. Well ...

Chuckles and pats LORENA'*s chair.*

Maybe not you. (*Beat.*) While we're on the
subject ...

Snaps her fingers and the lights come up.

There are many starving children in Africa. As
you can imagine, they don't have lots of good
things to eat like we have here. They don't have
milk to drink, or mashed potatoes, or grilled
cheese sandwiches on Wonderbread. They

sleep right on the floor in houses made of straw—that don't even have any walls—and drink out of the same watering holes with the zebras and crocodiles. Well. These poor children obviously need our help.

She takes an orange UNICEF *box from under the white material.*

That's why every year the good people at UNICEF ask nice Canadian children, like yourselves, to take this little box with them on Halloween and collect donations along with their trick-or-treats. The money you raise will be used to buy food, water, building materials and even a few schoolbooks for all the poor hungry people in Africa. So, don't forget to pick up your UNICEF box before you leave the school. In fact, I'll just leave one right here on Lorena's desk. A helpful reminder.

Now, where was I ...

II

The end of 'Soul Man' fades into ambient party sounds.

Slides—photos of people listening to music and of parties are shown throughout the scene.

LORENA

There are voices in the night. Dark voices. Warm as gingerbread and comfortingly familiar. It's Saturday night and the folks have come up from downtown. My uncles, my sister's school friends.

The sound of 'Grooving on a Sunday Afternoon' by The Young Rascals fades in.

And they've brought chicken from the Chalet Lucerne. I can smell it sweet and pungent through the stench of cigarette smoke. And in the morning there will be a wing, my favorite part, saved for me.

Listening.

The Young Rascals croon softly in the background "Grooving on a Sunday afternoon ... "

A male voice rises. A murmured female reply. Then the multi-pleasured laughter of a mellowed crowd's response. Some thing groooovy is going on and I want to be a part of it.

LORENA *sneaks toward the screen.*

Slide—image of a large door, slightly ajar.

VOICE OVER
A coloured man walks into a greasy spoon and sits at the lunch counter.
The waitress come over and says "Sorry we don't serve niggers here."
The colored man says "That's alright. I don't eat them."

LORENA
Laughter explodes like a raisin in the sun, rising beyond humor to an almost hysterical crescendo. Then diminishes into painful recognition. Followed by silence. Interminable and dense. And when they speak again, their tones are hushed and somber.

LORENA (*as a child*)
Listening at the 'door'.

There's a man with a dream ... and a woman on the bus ... and a young boy hanging from a tree ... the Panthers have left the jungle and have moved to the city ... 'cause there's a war overseas ... and coloured people are supposed

to be free! They say the days of slavery are over
... but the men in white hoods snatch you at
night! That's why Chicago's burning ... people
are sitting in Arkansas. people are sitting in
Alabama. Malcolm. No, Martin. No, Martin.
No, Malcolm. No, Martin is going to overcome.

> *Slide—(text flashes onto the screen, super-*
> *imposed on the image of the door, getting*
> *larger each time, repeatedly throughout the*
> *scene)*
> Change.

VOICE OVER (*female*)
When are we all going to be free?

> *Slide—(text)*
> Change.

LORENA (*as a child, frightened*)
Change.

VOICE OVER (*male*)
I remember when they wouldn't serve us in the
restaurants on St. Catherine's street Or let us
in the movie theatres ...

> *Slide—(text)*
> Change.

LORENA
Change.

VOICE OVER (*female*)
We have our rights.

Slide—(text)
Change.

LORENA
Change.

VOICE OVER (*female*)
Education is the key.

Slide—(text)
Change.

LORENA
Change.

VOICE OVER (*male*)
By any means necessary.

Slide—(text)
Change.

LORENA
Change.

VOICE OVER (*female*)
Yet lift me up!

VOICE OVER (*male*)
Hey. We could be doing a lot worse. We could
be living in the States. Or South Africa with
that apartheid shit. I'd say we're damned lucky
to be Canadians.

VOICE OVER (*female*)

> When was the last time you tried to get out of downtown?

VOICE OVER (*female*)

> Oh, that doesn't mean anything. We have the laws to protect us.

VOICE OVER (*male*)

> Yeah. At least we don't have to have to worry about crosses burning and getting lynched.

VOICE OVER (*female*)

> Amen.

VOICE OVER (*male*)

> But folks are dying in America. For our rights.

LORENA (*as a child*)

> (*Yawning*) The debate rages into the night. I fall asleep with my ear to the door.

> *Blackout.*

12

*In the black we hear bagpipes, feedback. The
sound of a voice on a public address system.*

ANNOUNCER (*voice over*)
Guy Drummond Elementary School proudly
presents ... Multicultural Day!

Lights come up.

ANNOUNCER (*voice over*)
From Scotland ...

LORENA *does a Highland Fling, smiles and
bows.*

ANNOUNCER (*voice over*)
From Israel ...

LORENA *dances the hora, smiles and bows.*

ANNOUNCER (*voice over*)
From Greece ...

LORENA *dances to 'Zorba the Greek', smiles
and bows.*

ANNOUNCER (*voice over*)
From China ...

LORENA *picks up mask of a dragon. Moves it around delicately, smiles and bows.*

LORENA (*as a child*)
  Look Ma! I fit!

13

Lights change. We hear eerie sounding music.

LORENA

A gang of kids waited for me in the schoolyard.
"What will you do, now that your leader is
dead?" they rumbled.

I ran home in fear of what they might do to me
and found my mother slumped over the
kitchen table crying.

LORENA (*as* LILLIAN)

They shot him. The bastards shot him. They
couldn't let an intelligent black man live. They
couldn't lynch him, so they shot him. They
shot him. Martin Luther King. They shot him
dead on the ground.

> *Slide—Photo of the assassination of Martin
> Luther King Jr., in which people are pointing
> from their balconies in horror.*

LORENA

Oh, God! Our leader is dead, and my mother is
moaning. I want to stop her tears, bring him
back to life, anything to keep my mother's
strength from crumbling before me. But she

wasn't crumbling. She was angry and the fierceness she had always kept hidden from me was like fire in her eyes.

LORENA (*as* LILLIAN)

Don't you ever trust the Whites. Don't you ever trust them. Every time you try to rise up, they'll beat you down again. They'll try to rob you of your dignity. They'll try to steal your pride. They'll take everything you have in this world just to keep you in your place. They'll even take your life. But there is one thing God gave you that's yours to keep forever, and they can't take that from you unless you give it up to them. I'm talking about your soul, Lorena. Don't ever give away your soul. You hear me? I'm talking about survival in the white man's world.

Don't let them break your spirit. Don't ever let them break you. If they knock you down, get up again. If they try to hold you back, just keep on pushing forward. Don't take no for an answer. Don't give up no matter how hard it gets. Just keep pounding on that door and some day it will open for you. Keep reaching for the stars and you'll have the universe.

We are coloured. And though your race will seem like a weight around your shoulders, don't let anybody tell you that you aren't beautiful and good. You are the future. You have a right to the future. Don't let anyone take that away from you.

LORENA

There was conviction in her voice and determination in the lines of her face. The dream that was Martin, that light on the periphery of my existence, flares in the heavens like a star turned nova and shines on me from my mother's eyes. They may have killed our leader, but they haven't killed our hope.

Bright white lights facing the audience flash
blindingly—a white out. Blackout.

Footlights come up, projecting Lorena's shadow
on the screen. The music fades into a dream-
like sound, the soft whistling of wind.

LORENA

... Je suis perdue dans une plaine de neige
aveuglante. Je me couvre les yeux des mains,
pour les protéger du soleil. Je regarde autour de
moi. J'ai besoin d'un repère pour me diriger.
Mais tout que je vois c'est le bleu et le blanc du
ciel et de la neige.

Je commence à croire que je vais mourir là.
Mon coeur et mon corps—complètement
congelés. Je vais être retrouvé là, ou je me
tiens, dans cette posture, comme une sculpture
en glace solitaire, exposé dramatiquement sur
une couche de neige.

Non. Je ne veux pas mourir comme ça. Il faut
que je trouve un moyen de sortir d'ici. Il faut
que je bouge.

Footlights fade to black.

15

We hear Aretha Franklin singing 'I need love, love, love'. LORENA sings along.

Slide—Photo of LORENA *as a teenager.*

Slide—(text superimposed on the photo of Lorena)
Oh Mama. Is anyone ever going to love me?

LORENA
Oh Mama. Is anyone ever going to love me?

LORENA (*as* LILLIAN)
There's plenty of time for that nonsense! You've got more important things to think about, like how you're going to get by in this world. If you spent more time worrying about your future than boys you might find yourself getting some place. And don't mess up your life by getting pregnant. Keep your skirt down and your legs crossed and stay away from white boys!

16

Slide—(text)
5 REASONS TO STAY AWAY FROM
WHITE BOYS.

*Jazz music. LORENA crosses to the screen
and reads the slides aloud.*

Slide—(text)
1–They only want one thing.
2–They don't commit to black girls.
3–They think all black women are whores.
4–They make promises the can't keep.
5–They won't respect you.

LORENA
But there are no black ones.

Slide—(text)
Amour.

LORENA

He says he loves me but he won't speak
English. He says, "Je t'aime, Loren. Je t'aime." I
want to believe him. But my name is Lorena.

He says he loves me but he won't speak
English. He's a vrai Péquist and won't dare to
speak a word of the language of his oppressor.
But the truth is my broken French is better
than his English and I think it embarrasses
him.

When we're with his friends, he speaks a rapid-
fire joual that's bewildering to follow. I try to
nod my head and laugh in the appropriate
spaces. But no one is fooled. Each exchange is
followed with "Comprends-tu?" Or explained in
baby syllables, "Il-a-dit-que- blah, blah, blah.
Comprends-tu?" And sometimes when I try to
contribute to the conversation, I'm told to, "Just
speak English." They say, "Tu parles français
comme une vache espanol."

But when we are alone, his breath hot upon my neck, he murmurs, "J'aurais toujours envie de te serer fort dans me bras." I hear, "I will always want that you claw hard in my arms ... "?! His words of love get lost in my kinky translations. Instead, I interpret the intimacy of his touch, the soft intensity in his eyes and abandon myself to the rhythms of his romantic language. I'm making love in French!

Then I understand that he will always want to hold me in his arms, because that is where I want to always be.

He says he loves me but he won't speak English. I turn to say I love you too. But check myself and say "Je t'aime." I want to say more but the words get scrambled in my mind. Les mots ne viens pas facilement.

> *Slide—(text)*
> Si tu veut parler en français il faut que tu penses en françias.

He says he loves me but he won't speak English. He wants to take me home! À Drummondville. Son endroit! I don't really want to go. My love life is like the lyrics of a Janis Ian song. I know what heartache lives along that road. Still we wind our way east along the St. Lawrence, through small towns with church spires gleaming white against a clear blue sky, meandering towards his history.

The farther from Montreal we travel the more conspicuous I feel. I see surprise in the faces of diners in the Casse Croute in St. Hyacinthe where we stop for lunch. Some sneak a peek at me between bites of hamburger steak and others gawk openly like I'm some strange and shameful beast. He is oblivious to my discomfort. Love is blind.

Traditional Quebecois folk music begins playing.

His folks are of vielle souche, les habitants, sturdy, unpretentious folk. Their faces warm and open. Omer, with belt buckle lost beneath his "grosse bédune" pumps my hand enthusiastically, "Bienvenue, bienvenue!" And Henriette, with her plain tan sweater buttoned devoutly to her neck, takes my face in both her hands and presses her lips to my cheeks. "Nous sommes trés content de te voir. Enfin. Marcel avais parlé beaucoup de toi. Vienne. Vienne t'assoire. Une place speciale pour toi."

"Henriette don't speak no Henglish. Me. I don't speak good Henglish but I try."

"Comme vous voulez. Je parle français. Pas tres bien mais j'essaye aussi."

And we laugh.

I am surprised. They want me to like them as much as I want them to like me.

Si tu veut penser en français, il faut que tu
vives en français.

He says he loves me but he won't speak
English. Big fucking deal! I am elated. He says
he loves me and he wants to live with me!

My Anglo friends complain they never see me
any more. They feel betrayed. But they don't
understand!

This language that I live in, this English I take
shit for each time I leave home, is not my
English! Each word's a link, each phrase a
chain that's forged in centuries of slavery. I
speak Massa's tongue. And though I've
mastered the language of my subjugation, I
still yearn for the authentic voices of the lost
generations of my ancestry. We share in spirit a
desire to preserve what's left of our shattered
identities. Side by side we'll fight the powers of
oppression and live as revolutionaries in the
struggle for social change. Together we will
smash the shackles of colonial domination.
Two niggers in America united by love. Free at
last. Free at last.Vive Québec libre! Free at last!

So I renounce my Anglo roots and move with
him into a four-room flat on Colonial and
Duluth.

We do the things that lovers do. Play in bed until two. Then crawl out into the afternoon sun, still entwined like differing plants that grow together, their leaves a tangle of familiarity. Inseparable. Windowshop on St. Denis and browse in bookstores along the way.

This book is far from ostentatious. No bold print or glossy cover screaming for a sale. But sepia toned and made to look like aged and faded paper. It is the doleful black face on the cover that rouses my curiosity and compels me to innocently pick it up and crack its spine.

They say a picture's worth a thousand words in any language.

Faint southern gospel singing is heard in the background.

It's not the smoldering remains of what had been a man that shocks me. His once black features charred beyond recognition. It is the twenty or thirty white men that stand behind the pyre, proudly arranged like graduates for a class picture.

Slides—different close-ups of the faces of respectable-looking white men in a crowd.

Their triumphant smiles. Their self-satisfied demeanor. Their total unconcern for the life they took, for that life was of no value to them except in macabre sport. Their shameless hatred. They didn't even bother to wear their hoods or robes.

Exposed and smiling for the camera, their eyes all seem to follow me. Pandora's book! I want to snap it shut but it's too late. I've been identified.

He says "Don't look. Loren. Don't look."

But I can't look away. I can't just look away.

Slides stop.

He says he loves me. Even in English sometimes. His sudden fluency surprises me. But it really doesn't matter what language he says it in. Each time we pass that bookstore I have to stop and look.

Each time he says, "Don't look Loren. Don't look. Why do you 'ave to look at that?"

These men, these men who think they are so great, they are so much better, these men are everywhere! I have to remember their faces. I forget sometimes who I am and where I ultimately come from. These men remind me that a lapse of memory could one day prove itself to be fatal. And I want him to look with me. It is important that he look with me.

Regard, Marcel. Regard. Quelle sort des hommes peuvent faire ca!?

Slide—the entire photograph of the respectable-looking white men is revealed. The crowd surrounds the charred remains of a lynched black man.

He says he loves me. He says "I love you Loren. I look at you and I see you. I don't see no color. Just Loren. And I love him. Her."

I want to believe him. But I am more than the languages I speak. Who I am is embedded in every cell of my skin. How can he love what he can't see? What he won't see?

18

We hear hot, restrained jazz; Dexter Gordon's 'Tanya'.

Slide—(text)
THE DISCOVERY OF WHAT IT MEANS
TO BE A CANADIAN

Slides—photos of the city at night, and angry, intense and despairing faces of black people throughout the scene.

LORENA

I was blind but now I see. I see it everywhere.
In the eyes of the "other" that seem to look
right through me as if I am not there. In the
eyes of the dark and dispossessed, red-rimmed
with watery rage suppressed and masked with
stoicism.

I see what my mother strove so hard to spare
me, prepare me for: a world that's quick to
judge a person solely on the basis of the color
of their skin and not on their merit. A world
where white is might and if you happen to be
born black—well, there's always room at the
back of the bus otherwise, step down.

And this world isn't south of anywhere. It's north. True north. Strong and free. But for only the fair.

I walk ...

> Slide—*(text)*
> TO BE BLACK AND ENLIGHTENED IN TODAY'S SOCIETY IS TO BE IN A CONSTANT STATE OF RAGE.

... unemployed and almost homeless. Through streets of slushy grey, raining grey rain from a grey sky. Relying on the kindness of strangers and finding most are all too familiar in their response.

I see—

> LORENA *claps her hands and turns her head as if slapped in the face.*

—why each apartments just been rented when I show up for a viewing! I see—

> *Claps again and reacts as if slapped.*

—why the perfect candidate just precedes me at each job interview! Is it my stomach rumbling? Or the awakening anger within?

I walk ...

Like a target though these streets.

Past scores of Haitian cabbies, fired from the
SOS Cab Company for being what they cannot
change.

Past three middle-aged black women on their
way home from church, being frisked by the
police because they are suspect, suspected of
being ...

Past Anthony Griffin, gunned down by the
authorities and lying in a pool of his own
innocence and blood.

There's Ruben Francois,
Black Snow Goat,
waiting on the corner of Crescent and St.
Catherines
with a can of gasoline in one hand
and a book of his self published poems in the
other.
There's fire in his heart
though his smile is serene.
Anointing himself like Buddhist priest,
he calls to me ...

LORENA (*as* RUBEN)
When the weight of life is on your shoulder,
Sister, don't show any sadness on your face
for no one will pity you. Oh, look at me now!

LORENA
He calls to me ...

LORENA (*as* RUBEN)
 Get up and fight!
 It's everybody's everything.

LORENA
 He calls to me ...

LORENA (*as* RUBEN)
 By god, I light the candle, burn the incense
 the smoke in my head, a hole in my soul
 proudly, walk I the streets in my search to be
 free
 the spirit by my side, someday soon
 you will know what I mean!

LORENA
 He calls.
 Then sets himself ablaze in protest.

 And I walk ...
 Past "white only" restaurants,
 and "white only" taxi stands,
 and "white only" apartment buildings,
 and "white only" night clubs
 and I see the unlegislated signs of segregation.
 Subtle and tacitly agreed upon.
 Unspoken
 in two official languages.

 *Slides—Photos of Malcolm X and Martin Luther
 King Jr. flash through images of fire.* LORENA *sits
 upstage with her back to the audience for about a
 minute while the music plays out.*

19

LORENA (as ETHEL, a West Indian Woman)
I am tired, Lo. So tired of all dis French/
English bullshit! Day in, day out. Dey threaten'
to close the hospital, you know? Notice is only
the English one dey threaten. Dey layin' off
people left and right. I lucky I still got me job.
But I puttin' in double shift every other day.
Some days me so tired I just see white.

But I ain't complainin'. I take every hour dey
see fit to give me. I savin' my pennies. Because
I know for you and me is not about French or
English.

Here's what happened. I just finished putting
in a double shift: 11 to 7, 7 to 3. All I want to do
is go home and curl up in me bed, but I got to
take de boy to de dentist. So I rush like hell
from de hospital, grab de boy from his school
and race clip clip to de dentist's office.

Now, I don't recognize de receptionist. But I
don't pay it no mind. Dey change dese girls
sometimes more often than dey change dheir
undershorts. Dis one, skinny black haired
thing. She on de phone talking away and we

66

stand standing dhere. We wait and we wait. Five minutes pass and we still standing dhere.

Finally she looks up at me and say, "What you want?"

I say, "We have an appointment at 3.30. Sorry we're a bit late."

She say, "That's impossible."

I say, "What you mean I don't have an appointment. My name is Ethel Martin. It could be under my son's name Rasheed."

She say, "No. You have no appointment here."

Now me tinkin' what de hell's going on here? I take de appointment slip out of me pocket. I say, "But see. It says 3.30. Monday. The 27th."

She say, "I told you. That's not here."

You know dhese office buildings everyting looks de same? De same white reception counter, de same orange chairs in de waitin' area. De same damn pictures of happy teeth on de walls. Noting but dis bitch to tell me is different. I was on de wrong floor. How was I to know dhere was another dentist office directly below my own? I suppose I could have looked at de name on de door but I didn't. I was tired and in a hurry. It was a mistake. An honest mistake. Anyone could have made it.

So, me and de boy go leave and under her breath she says, "Stupid."

I don't know why I didn't let it slide. But I stop and turn around to her and I say, "You know. You are very rude."

And she come out from behind de counter, all red face, shouting, "You black bitch! You get out of here!" And she shoves me through de doorway!

Now me feet ain't caught up wit' me body. I still got one in se office. She slam de door on my foot so hard de glass panel crack. And if dhat was not enough of an assault on my person, she follows me into de hall with her "stupid dis" and "black dat" and "go back where you came from" and hitting on me and pushing me around.

I look at me boy. His eyes wide and shiny. I never seen him look so scared. He's moving back and forth like so. He's saying, "Mommy, Mommy let's go Mommy." But dis crazy bitch won't let me go. And then she turn and raise her hand to strike my child. Well, I just pulled back me fist and popped her one in de face! Grabbed de boy's hand and went on about my business.

After his appointment, we step out of de building and dhat bitch is dhere wit' de police.

"C'est elle!" she yells. And de next ting I know, I am being arrested for assault. Dey handcuff me hands behind me back like I'm some dangerous criminal. Rummage trough me hand bag. Feel me up and down, so, like I got some deadly weapon up underneath me uniform. Right dhere on de street! And dey shove me and de boy in de back seat of de police car and take us to de station. All dat. All dat humiliation and degradation. Right in front of me child's eyes!

I don't go to court for a few months yet. You know dey wanting me to pay for de replacement of de glass panel dat bitch crack on me foot! De lawyer ain't worried. Plenty people waiting in the office. Good people willing to testify on my behalf.

But I tell you someting. When dis nightmare is over, I am packing up me things and taking me boy to Toronto. How can I teach him to have respect for people who have no respect for him? If it's like dis now, what it goin' to be like when dey got dey own country, huh? I am forty-five years old. Ain't noting worth living out de rest of my life like shit on the sole of a Frenchman's shoe.

You damn right. I'm getting the hell out of here!

White out.

Footlights come up, projecting LORENA*'s shadow on the screen.*

LORENA

Il faut que je trouve un moyen de sortir d'ici. Il faut que je bouge.

Au loin, très loin, il y a quelques chose à peine perceptible. Un tout petit point noir ou le ciel et la neige s'embrassent à l'horizon.

Un tronc d'arbre peut-être. Une roche.

Pas à pas, je marche vers ce point. Mes yeux baissé, une tête basse contre les rayons de soleil. Je marche ... pas d'empreinte dans la neige! Lentement, mais avec détermination. Il me semble que plus je marche, plus loin est la destination. Que je ne vais jamais y arriver. Mais c'est du mouvement et ca me réchauffe et je retrouve mon espoir.

Slide—Photo of Lillian, her hands covering her face.

Slide—(text, beginning small and growing larger throughout the scene, flashing across the image of Lillian)
Go ...

VOICE OVER
Go ...

LORENA
We are sitting on her balcony at the Rockhill Apartments. The sun rolls down the slopes of Mont Royal cemetery and dances off the crystalline patches of melting snow, tender green shoots of new spring grass and the glistening headstones of the gone but not forgotten.

Bundled like a baby in Hudson's Bay blankets, she complains about the cold and dampness. Despite her discomfort, I insist that we stay outside for a little while longer. She rarely leaves the apartment anymore and needs the fresh air.

Slide—(text)
Go ...

VOICE OVER
Go ...

LORENA
You would not know that she is fifty-seven to look at her. She still looks like she could be my sister and I am the youngest of five adult children. It is her hands that reveal her internal age, which is about seventy-five. Her clothes disguise the rest.

Slide—(text)
Go ...

VOICE OVER
Go ...

LORENA
These hands ... These hands have large misshapen knuckles and fingers that are crippled, bending at the joints every which way. Her 'zeds' she calls them in an attempt at humour. But mostly she tries to keep them hidden from view.

Slide—(text)
Go ...

VOICE OVER
Go ...

LORENA *rests her head on the chair.*

LORENA
> I drop to my knees and rest my head in her lap.
> And despite the pain I know she feels, she
> takes one of these hands and smooths back my
> hair, caresses my brow.
>
> I say, "Oh Mama is anybody ever gonna love
> me?"
>
> She says, "I love you."
>
> I say,"Oh Maw. That's not what I mean ... "
>
> "You have plenty of time for that nonsense,"
> she says.
>
> "But you've been saying that to me since I was
> fourteen years old."
>
> She takes a lock of my hair in her crooked
> fingers and tickles my ear, like when I was
> child and she wanted to wake me. But I am
> awake and a woman now.
>
> > *Slide—(text)*
> > Go ...

VOICE OVER
> Go ...

LORENA
> I say, "I've been thinking Maw. Wht if that
> person that's meant for only me isn't in
> Montreal? Lord knows I've worn my heart out
> searching the city for them. What if they are

somewhere else in the world? Just waiting to meet me. It's possible ... "

"Anything is possible," she says, "If you believe."

And one of these hands attempts to squeeze my shoulder reassuringly.

I say, as conversationally as possible, "You know Lisa's gone to Vancouver."

She says, "Uh huh ... "

I say, "Yeah. Louise is in Ottawa. And Brenda just got this great job in Toronto. Pretty soon I won't have any friends left here at all."

"Have you found a job yet?" she asks.

"No," I say "but I'm okay for a few months. Something will happen soon."

And for the longest time these hands sit silent and heavy on my shoulders ...

"Go," she says. "Go to the farthest place. And work your way back. If you have to. You can always come back if you have to."

But how, in good conscience, can I leave these hands? These hands that slapped and nursed me? That played the 'Moonlight Sonata' and delighted in braiding my hair? These hands can no longer carry a Steinberg's bag, button a blouse, pick a dime from a change purse or brush her still black and lustrous hair. These hands. How can I leave these aching hands? How can I leave these hands when they obviously need me so?

As if reading my thoughts she adds, "As long as I am here you will always have a home to come back to. So go. Go. Don't worry about me. I'll be just fine. I have survived this long haven't I?"

I put my arms around her waist and bury my face in her lap. The osteoarthritis is all through her body and though it pains her to be held, she endures my embrace. I smell her through the blankets. The smell beneath her perfume. Her smell. I love her smell. How can I leave her smell?

She pats me on the back and laughs, "I'll help you pack."

And then these hands release me, like a thousand yellow butterflies fluttering goodbye.

LORENA, *kneeling by the chair, waves goodbye.*

22

The sound of an airplane. LORENA *retrieves a black and white umbrella from under the white material. She raises the umbrella.*

Slides—rainy Vancouver scenes and people with umbrellas.

LORENA

Rainrain rain rain rainrain rain rain rain rain rain rainrain ...

Dear Louise,

Greetings from soggy Vancouver! It has been raining for eight days straight and the streets are covered in slugs. Brown slimy things, not unlike long runny turds that ooze along the sidewalk. The streets are just slithering with them. Really gross.

I can't believe it's been three months already. It feels like for fucking ever.

I have moved out of my sister's windowless basement in Surrey, into a one bedroom apartment in the downtown west end. There's nothing in it except my bed. But it's three blocks from English Bay, and I have developed a fondness for sitting on the beach and "watching the ships roll in"—just like in that Otis Redding song. Yes girl, Lorena on the beach! I'm doing nature! (You can't avoid it out here. It's fuckin' everywhere!) Mind you, I am going to have to get appropriate footwear. My heels keep getting stuck in the sand.

I got myself a little job at an all night depanneur, excuse me, convenience store about four blocks from where I live. I had a job in market research, but I got fired when I didn't show on June 24. I said, "Hey it's St. Jean Baptiste Day. A holiday." They said, "Not here it ain't." And gave me the boot! It's just as well. I was getting tired calling people and asking them intimate questions about their feminine protection.

So, how's life in Ottawa? Capitol punishment? I don't know about you but I am finding it hard adjusting to life in Canada. First of all people don't know how to dress here. Everyone looks like they just crawled out of a kayak or some other outdoorsy thing. Bush bunnies. They wear big cloddy boots all the time. (The better to stomp slugs with I guess.) I find I am overdressed for just about every occasion. And I can't even dress properly because there's not one place in the whole fucking city that sells flesh-coloured pantyhose the color of my flesh!

I won't even talk about make-up or hair products.

There are no black people in Vancouver. I can go for days where the only black face I see is my reflection in a store window. And when I do see another black person I stop and try to flag them down.

Everything shuts down at one A.M. like some fucking temperance colony. You can buy pornography at the corner store but not beer and wine. (Figure that one.) And people get in your face for just about everything; for smoking cigarettes, for swearing, for waving your hands and raising your voice when you get excited. Don't get passionate and above all, don't get political. It's like there is some law against having a good time here. The B.C. No Fun Laws. They are really frustrating.

And English! It' so omnipresent. Did you know that the STOP signs actually say STOP!? In big bold white letters?! And nothing else!? Is it like that everywhere in Canada? Everywhere unilingual English signs. It's creepy.

And I don't understand this English. Back home, you were Italian, you were Greek, Polish, Hungarian, Dahomian, whatever, you spoke English, it was an agreement. A way of establishing common bonds. You were a part of something. It made you feel like a revolutionary. But here, they use it to bludgeon people with. Particularly immigrants. They say, "You're in Canada now. Speak English!" And there is actually a group called "The Society for the Preservation of the English Language." It probably just a bunch of old Brits sitting around eating mushy peas and singing Rule Britannia. But still, it's offensive. I feel like I just traded one kind of language prejudice for another.

I got a call from Peter. He's thinking of moving out here. And do you remember Leslie? She lives just two apartments down from me. I keep running into all kinds of folks from home. Every day there's a new batch of refugees—French and English. It's funny, in Montreal none of us would give each other the time of day but here ... we cling to each other. There's a gang of about twenty of us expatriates. We get together every so often to eat and a drink and smoke and talk and swear real loud. Hell, we even speak French and we don't have to, anymore. We go to restaurants that promise a taste of home—Montreal-style bagels and Montreal-style smoked meat and Montreal-style barbecued chicken. We have come to the conclusion that there's a pokey little town somewhere in Missouri named Montreal, 'cause we ain't et anything in Montreal, Quebec that tastes this shitty.

The one thing we've learned living here is that we may all speak English but we're sure as hell not Anglos. No matter what Bourassa or Parizeau or any of them say, we are Quebecois! And we each feel out of place in Canada, in our own way.

I miss Montreal. And I want to go home. But can't 'cause I promised my mother I'd give it a year. Three months down, nine to go. Meanwhile, rain rain rain rain rain rain rain.

Write soon. And if you get back to Montreal, tell her I love her.

Your friend,

Lorena

PS. I almost forgot. I met a man.

23

Flashing disco party lights and dance music,
LORENA *dances and imagines she is eating*
food.

LORENA (*voice over*)
Steamies at Montreal Pool room.
Smoked meat Schwartz's.
Schuller's kosher barbecue potato chips.
Cott's Black Cherry soda, 'cause if it's Cott it's
got to be good!
Dry garlic spareribs at the Dragon Inn on
Decarie.
Cream cheese party sandwiches from the
Snowdon Deli.
Orange Tarts at Café Castillo on Sherbrooke by
The Cinema Five.
Sunday brunch at Les Filles du Roi.
Praline and Ice cream crepes at Le Petit Halle.
Hamburgers and french fries at Lafleurs.
The lobster festival at Amazona's on Côte St. Luc.
Bagels from the Bagel Factory on Fairmont
Pineapple chicken at Lung Fungs.
BarB Barn Ribs.
A cabane à sucre breakfast with scrambled
eggs, baked beans, back bacon, home fries, and
tortierre.

Chicken at the Chalet Barbecue.
Onion Baji's at the Star of India.
Blueberry cheese cake at Le Commençal.

LORENA
I crave the flavors of my past and long to taste
again the city that I love to eat. I will devour
Montreal, savoring each sweet and sour
memory that bursts upon my tongue. I will
dine at eight, and until three, I'll gorge myself
with reverie and laugh again with those I loved!

I'm going home. Home. Where the heart is.
Where the hate is. Where the have to, hard to,
happy to is. The prodigal daughter returns with
a hunger.

LORENA (*voice over*)
Chocolate cake at Fridays.
Pendelli's Pizza.
Coquilles St. Jacques and profiteroles at Chez
Delmos on Notre Dame.
Three fish terrine at La Rapiere.
Hot polish sausage at the Café Prague.

Slide—triplex house at 6180 Durocher.

LORENA
6180 Durocher still stands.
And though the filmy white curtains
have been many times replaced
with those of other styles,
by those of other tastes,

the long glass door panels
still gleam
invitingly.
I dare not ring the bell
and ask to mount those steps
again.
I've crossed that threshold many times.
Let other lives
play out their mundane dramas
between those walls.
I am content
to stand outside
imagining
the secret and familiar spaces
I once knew
to be mine.

Slide—Schwartz's restaurant.

Schwartz's is still packed
and spicy smelling!
Pickled peppers
medium fat
double mustard
greasy fingers
slipping
on the cold tin
of my black cherry pop.

Slide—Chalet Barbecue.

And lunch at Chalet Barbecue
is still the cheapest deal in town.

But Cafe Prague ... gone.

Slide—the images comes up empty, just white light. Repeated throughout the scene.

Dragon Inn—gone.

Slide—(empty).

Star of India—gone.

Slide—(empty).

Cafe Castillo—gone.

Slide—(empty).

La Petite Halle—gone.

Slide—(empty).

Lung Fung's—gone.

Slide—(empty).

Finast's—gone.

Slide—(empty).

Frank's—gone.

Slide—(empty).

Strathcona Academy—gone.

Slide—(empty).

Guy Drummond—gone.

Slide—(empty).

Each pilgrimage finds that Mecca's disappeared
without a forwarding address.

*Slide—store window with 'à louer' and 'à
vendre' signs.*

St. Catherine Street feels empty.
The hollow eyed store windows,
once dazzling with bargains,
stare blankly behind
À louer and
À vendre
signs.

Slide—Peel and St. Catherine's streets.

I stand
on the corner of Peel and St. Catherine,
at five P.M. on Thursday,
waiting for the light to change,
feeling cramped
by the buildings
that I'm seeing for the first time
without
their payday crowds.
I cross the street
alone.

Slide—Grumpy's Bar.

I delight at finding
Grumpy's

still downstairs.
But my once nightly retreat
no longer feels jazzy
nor exclusive
with its pub style
renovations
and my booze buddies have all
moved on
in body and in spirit
or aged
beyond my recognition.
I drink a toast
to the echoing
"last call" laughter
of my past
and leave
drunk
with disappointment.

Montreal and I have changed.
She does not bear
the weight of
her depression well.
But sags
like baggy stockings
around
an old woman's ankles.
And I have become accustomed to
green
Westcoast surroundings.

"Go to the farthest place
and work your way back ...
if you have to.
You can always come home ...
if you have to,"
my mother said.
But even she is gone.

24

Slide—interior of Joe's Café.

LORENA

> *(speaking directly to the audience)* And this is
> what I was going to tell my friend before I was
> so rudely interrupted. I had gone to Montreal
> to visit my mother's grave. It had been three
> heartbroken years since she died. I needed, not
> only to make my peace with her, but to make
> sure that she'd been buried in the right spot.
>
> You see, my mother never liked the heat. And
> some graves are right out there in the open. I
> didn't want her sweating in the sun for all
> eternity. So I specifically requested a shady plot
> beneath the tree. But she died in January. The
> tree was naked and spindly. And I guess the
> ground was too frozen to turn because when I
> left the cemetery her casket was still sitting out
> on one of those portable folding tables on the
> spot designated for her burial. The ground
> hadn't even been broke. For all I knew she was
> still sitting out there.
>
> I needed the closure of seeing that she had
> been committed to the ground.

Now, my mother was buried in Memorial Park Cemetery in Ville St. Laurent. My friend Andrew offered to drive me. And though I had the vague recollection of the cemetery being on Côte de Liesse just past the National Film Board, I thought to check the address before we left.

So I look in the White Pages and it's not there. I look in the Yellow Pages and it's not there either. I think ok. You're in Quebec now. Translate. I look under Parc Memorial. Nothing. Cemetaire Memorial. Nada. I call the information operator and she insists there is no such listing.

Now I am really in a panic. A whole fucking cemetery can't just just get up and walk away. Where the hell is my mother!!?

We hop in the car, drive up Cremazie, onto the Metropolitan, exit on Côte Liesse ... and bam! The one-eyed guy and the NFB are right where I remember 'em. We drive a little further and come to the high stone walls of the cemetery. It too is just where I remember it.

I'm thinking "Now, what the Hell just happened there?" Maybe the cemetery just got filled up and stopped advertising. We'll drive up to the gates and see a red neon sign flashing "No Vacancy" or "Standing Room Only."

We see a sign alright and it is not amusing. It says "Les Jardins Urgel Bourgie."

Les Jardins Urgel Bourgie! That's no translation for Memorial Park! Les Jardin Urgel Bourgie! It's an Urgel Bourgie Cemetery! They sold the fucking cemetery to Urgel Bourgie!

Urgel Bourgie is a large French undertaking company. My mother hated them! She always said "I've had to live my life in French. I want to die in English. Stick me in an English cemetery like Memorial Park. And no matter how cheap it is, don't let those Urgel Bourgie people touch me." And now she's decomposing in the shadow of their sign. I hear her cursing in her grave.

They could have, at least, informed me of their intent to sell. I would like to have had the chance to voice my opinion on their decision. Or at least given my consent. But this was decided independently of me, like so many decisions being made in and around Quebec.

I found my mother right where I left her. Only six feet under. And it was as I requested—a quiet shady spot beneath a spreading maple tree. I sat a moment and contemplated her epitaph: "Too well loved to be forgotten." I noticed at least a half a dozen other grave stones in her immediate vicinity that bore the same inscription. There must have been a sale that year. "To well loved to be forgotten." Aw, ma. How could I ever forget?

White out.

25

Footlights come up, projecting Lorena's shadow on the screen.

LORENA

Je retrouve l'espoir. Et soudainement, ma lueur est là, en face de moi.

Et je trouve que ce point à l'horizon blanc n'est pas une roche ni un tronc d'arbre. Mais une femme, noire et toute nue dans la neige. Je ne peux pas voir son visage—son dos est tourné vers moi. Mais je sais qu'elle n'était pas aveuglé par les rayon do soleil ni gené le froid.

Elle ce tient toute droite sa tête—haute et fière. Ses mains—placé hautainement sur les hanches—et les pieds plantées solidement sur terre.

Elle a l'air complètement chez elle, indifférent à cet environnement hostile.

Qui est cette femme qui défie les elements et ose revendiquer cet endroit pour elle-même?

Je s'approche lentement et pose la main sur son épaule. Ma main tremble. J'ai peur. Elle

s'est tourné vers moi et je réalise alors qu'elle
est moi.

C'est moi!

Et je me réveille.

Blackout.

26

Lights come up. LORENA *places the chair back in its original position. Music is playing:* LORENA *singing 'Une Québécoise errante' (recorded).*

LORENA

On Oct. 30, 1995, I felt as if I'd come dangerously close to being severed from both my personal and family histories. And Pariseau's remarks regarding "pûr laine" and "ethnics" made it clear that the years and generations my family has invested in Québec were perceived to be of no consequence or value. We would never be accepted as Québecois. Because we are black and English-speaking, we did not have the right to love Quebec, to speak to that love, or to vote for it.

When I moved to Canada I did not stop being a Quebecoise. I discovered that I had always been one. I did not forfeit my identity. I gained it.

I am expatriate anglophone, Montréaliase, Québecoise. These are just a few of the memories of a life I lived in the land of my birth. I cannot be separated from them. They cannot be legislated out of being. Nor can the Supreme Court rule on their validity. They are a part of the distinct whole that is me.

Memory serves me.
An exile
in Canada.

Blackout.

The End